AQA AS UNIT 1

Accounting

Introduction to Financial Accounting

Ian Harrison

Philip Allan Updates, an imprint of Hodder Education, part of Hachette UK, Market Place, Deddington, Oxfordshire OX15 0SE

Orders
Bookpoint Ltd, 130 Milton Park, Abingdon, Oxfordshire OX14 4SB
tel: 01235 827720
fax: 01235 400454
e-mail: uk.orders@bookpoint.co.uk
Lines are open 9.00 a.m.–5.00 p.m., Monday to Saturday, with a 24-hour message answering service. You can also order through the Philip Allan Updates website: www.philipallan.co.uk

© Philip Allan Updates 2008

ISBN 978-0-340-95818-6

First printed 2008
Impression number 5 4 3 2 1
Year 2013 2012 2011 2010 2009 2008

This guide has been written specifically to support students preparing for the AQA AS Accounting Unit 1 examination. The content has been neither approved nor endorsed by AQA and remains the sole responsibility of the author.

Typeset by Phoenix Photosetting, Chatham, Kent
Printed by MPG Books, Bodmin

Hachette UK's policy is to use papers that are natural, renewable and recyclable products and made from wood grown in sustainable forests. The logging and manufacturing processes are expected to conform to the environmental regulations of the country of origin.

Contents

Introduction

About this guide 4

Aims of the AS qualification 4

Assessment 4

Content Guidance 6

Revision techniques 6

■ ■ ■

Content Guidance

About this section 10

Purposes of accounting 11

Accounting records 11

Verification of accounting records 15

Trading and profit and loss accounts and balance sheets 23

■ ■ ■

Questions and Answers

About this section 32

Q1 Source documents and subsidiary books 33

Q2 Subsidiary books and ledger accounts 35

Q3 Trading and profit and loss accounts and balance sheets 40

Q4 The cash book 45

Q5 The trial balance 47

Q6 Verifying accounting records: correcting errors 54

Q7 Verifying accounting records: preparing control accounts 57

Q8 Verifying accounting records: bank reconciliation statements 60

Q9 Trading and profit and loss accounts and balance sheets 64

Q10 Effect of errors on profit calculations 69

Introduction

About this guide

This student guide is an ideal resource for your revision of AQA Accounting AS Unit 1: Introduction to Financial Accounting.

The guide is in three sections:
- This **Introduction** covers the aims and assessment of AS and outlines study strategies and revision techniques.
- **Content Guidance** covers the content of Unit 1.
- **Questions and Answers** provides ten questions; each question focuses on a specific area of content. Each question is based on the format of the AS examination papers and is followed by two sample answers (an A-grade and lower-grade response) together with comments by the examiner.

You should read the relevant topic area in the Content Guidance section before you attempt a question from the Questions and Answers section. Only read the specimen answers after you have attempted the question yourself.

Aims of the AS qualification

The AS accounting course aims to encourage you to develop:
- an understanding of the importance of effective accounting information systems and an awareness of their limitations
- an understanding of the purposes, principles, concepts and techniques of accounting
- the transferable skills of numeracy, communication, ICT, application, presentation, interpretation, analysis and evaluation in an accounting context
- an appreciation of the effects of economic, legal, ethical, social, environmental and technological influences on accounting decisions
- a capacity for methodical and critical thought which serves as an end in itself as well as a basis for further study of accounting and other subjects

Assessment

Remember that the course is designed to allow you to show your ability and to use your skills. AS, as well as A2, papers assess the following assessment objectives in the context of the specification content and skills. The following assessment objectives are tested in all examination papers to varying degrees:
- **knowledge and understanding** of the accounting principles, concepts and techniques within familiar and unfamiliar situations

- **application** of knowledge and understanding to familiar and unfamiliar situations
- **analysis and evaluation** by ordering, interpreting and analysing information using an appropriate format — making judgements, decisions and recommendations after assessing alternative courses of action

Quality of written communication (QWC)

On each paper, 4 marks are awarded for the quality of written communication. The marks are split equally between written communication (for prose answers) and quality of presentation (for numerical answers). These marks are awarded in specific questions that are clearly identified on the examination paper.

The specification requires that you use:
- text that is legible, and that your spelling, punctuation and grammar ensure that the meaning is clear
- a form and style of writing that is appropriate to the purpose and to the complex subject matter
- information in a clear and coherent way, and that specialist vocabulary is used where appropriate

Unit 1

The approximate weightings for Unit 1 are:

Knowledge and understanding	40%	29 marks
Application	50%	39 marks
Analysis and evaluation	10%	8 marks
	100%	76 marks (plus 4 marks for QWC)

The bulk of the marks available in Unit 1 are for the lower-level skills of knowledge, understanding and application (68 marks), while only 8 marks are allocated for the higher-level skills of analysis and evaluation.

You can learn to recognise the marks allocated to the skills of analysis and evaluation by the use of certain 'trigger' words. The most common trigger words are:
- **Advise** — suggest solutions to a problem and justify your solution.
- **Analyse** — identify the characteristics of the information given.
- **Assess** — make an informed judgement based on information supplied in the question.
- **Discuss** — present advantages and disadvantages or strengths and weaknesses of a particular line of action and arrive at a conclusion based on the question scenario.
- **To what extent** — similar to 'discuss' but requiring a judgement based on the likelihood of the potential outcomes and effects on the given scenario.

It is important that answers requiring analysis and evaluation result in a judgement being made. You use these skills almost every day. For example, you might say to friends, 'Let's have a McDonald's for lunch because...' — that is a judgement. You might add to that an analysis: '...because it is closer than Starbucks' or '...because there is a good offer at McDonald's at the moment'.

Content Guidance

The Content Guidance section of this guide outlines the topic areas covered in Unit 1.

Unit 1 is designed as the foundation for the whole A-level course and covers double-entry procedures applied to the accounting systems of sole traders. It deals with how the double-entry system operates and will help you to develop your skills in keeping accounting records.

On completion of the unit you should be able to:
- record a variety of transactions in the double-entry system from source documents and the appropriate subsidiary books and demonstrate an understanding of the double-entry process
- transfer appropriate amounts from the nominal accounts in the general ledger and prepare a balance sheet in good form from the real accounts and any other relevant accounts
- make adjustments for prepayments and accruals both in the general ledger and to the final accounts
- make provision for depreciation in the profit and loss account and balance sheet using the straight-line method
- verify the accuracy of accounting records and explain the purpose of using verification techniques and appreciate any limitations on their uses
- assess the effect that errors have on profit calculations and on the relevant sections of a balance sheet

Revision techniques

Studying and revising for any examination should not be a last-minute desperate measure. In order to pass the examination you should make notes throughout your course. In accounting it is important that you practise questions based on each topic area on a regular basis.

There are certain layouts that you must learn — for example, there is no other way to remember the format of a trading account or a profit and loss account or a balance sheet.

Revision is a continuous process. Plan your revision well in advance and undertake it on a regular basis. Your teacher will have helped you in this process by setting homework and by giving regular tests in class time. Both these types of work are a valuable part of your revision programme. Use them to ensure that you do understand a topic covered in the homework or a test. Revise the topic to be covered in the test or homework before you do it. When your work is returned, note carefully your teacher's comments and try to put right any basic errors pointed out. If there are issues that you do not understand, ask your teacher to explain while the problem is still fresh in your mind.

Use each piece of work to build up a bank of knowledge and skills that you may be able to apply to subsequent pieces of work. As a subject, accounting is rather like a detective solving a crime; the pieces of information collected some weeks ago might help to solve today's problem.

There is no best way of revising. All students are different and you must find the methods that suit you best.

However, you must *learn* the key concepts in each topic area. This is usually easier than you might first think; the difficult part is applying the knowledge to the questions set by the examiner.

Draw up a revision programme well before your examination. Draw up a weekly plan that identifies a number of instances when you can devote an hour of uninterrupted time to your revision (switch off your mobile). Remember that, for most students, accounting will not be the only subject for revision — take this into account when making your plans.

Try to find the times of day that best suit you. If you are at school or college, try to use your free time during the day for revision — this will free up time in the evening when you may wish to see friends. Build this into your plans. In school or college find a quiet place in the library or in a spare classroom. You may not like working in a quiet atmosphere but it will be quiet in the examination hall.

Once you have drawn up your programme, try to stick to it. A regular routine will work best and pay the greatest dividends. If you lose concentration while revising, take a break. Alternatively, revise another topic or subject.

Varying your method of revision should help you to concentrate for longer periods of time. Try using some of the following:
- Read aloud.
- Explain topics to yourself.
- Test yourself.
- Use a friend and test each other.
- Use a friend to bounce ideas or answers off (take care that this technique does not end up as a gossip session).
- Summarise answers to written questions.
- Practise parts of questions that build up to a whole question.
- Practise questions under quiet examination conditions.

Ask yourself the question: 'Could I explain this topic to my uncle (who knows nothing about accounting)?' If you can honestly answer 'yes', you probably understand the topic and the topic only needs to be read through several times during revision. If your answer is 'no', you need to spend more time thoroughly revising the topic.

Use these tips as a basis for your revision programme:

- Revise only one topic at each of your revision sessions.
- When you get nearer to the examination date, try to extend the amount of time spent revising; you may have back-to-back examinations in one session.
- Read this guide and use your textbook plus your class notes to build up a comprehensive body of knowledge in each topic area. Make notes of the key points.
- Attempt the questions provided in the Questions and Answers section of this guide. Check your answers against the example answers provided. Read the examiner comments to find how the candidates could have improved their answers.
- Remember, like an athlete training for the Olympic Games, you have been training for these examinations for some time. Don't miss out on a good result through lack of training (revision).

Content
Guidance

This section of the guide outlines the topic areas of Unit 1. They are:

- purposes of accounting
- source documents and subsidiary books
- double entry
- verification of accounting records
- suspense accounts
- bank reconciliation statements
- control accounts
- trading and profit and loss accounts
- balance sheets
- bad debts

Purposes of accounting

Reasons for keeping accounting records

The owners or managers of businesses keep accounting records in order to record:
- incomes and expenditures during an accounting period
- profits and losses during an accounting period
- the value of and any changes in the values of assets and liabilities
- amounts owed to creditors and amounts owed by debtors and any changes to these amounts during an accounting period

Additionally, records are kept to allow interpretation and comparison of results over different time periods:
- to satisfy legal requirements, for example Revenue and Customs
- to allow any providers of finance to see that the capital they have invested is being used wisely and is in safe hands

All the above reasons can be summarised under the headings of stewardship and management.

Accounting records

Source documents and subsidiary books

Source documents

The financial recording process always starts with a source document. The source document is used to provide the first entry (the 'prime' entry) in the financial records. It is important that you are able to describe the details shown on each source document and the purpose for its issue. You should also be able to write up the appropriate subsidiary book from each type of source document.

The source documents are:
- **purchases invoice** — the document received from a credit supplier demanding payment. It also stipulates any credit terms.
- **sales invoice** — the document sent to a credit customer demanding payment. It also stipulates any credit terms.
- **cheque counterfoils** (cheque book 'stubs') — the record of the details entered on a cheque.
- **paying-in slip counterfoils** — the record of the details entered on the paying-in slip.

- **cash receipts** — the document showing that a certain amount of money has been paid.
- **till rolls** — the record made by a cash register showing all receipts.
- **bank statements** — these also act as a source document. The information provided by bank statements includes:
  - **standing orders** — instructions written by a bank customer asking the bank to pay a fixed amount of money on a regular basis into another account.
  - **direct debits** — these allow a business to charge costs to a customer's bank account automatically. The amount can be increased or decreased within certain limits agreed by the customer.
  - **BACS** (Bank Automated Clearing System)
  - **credit transfers**
- **bank charges** — the charges made by the bank for carrying out work for a customer.

It is important that you can define each of these terms concisely and know how they affect the business's bank balance.

Subsidiary books

There are six subsidiary books that could figure in an examination question. Remember that the subsidiary books are not part of the double-entry system, with the exception of the cash book.

The **journal proper** (often referred to as **journal**) is used, at this stage of your studies, for four types of transaction. It is used to record:
- the purchase of fixed assets on credit terms
- the sale of fixed assets on credit terms
- the transfer of entries from one ledger account to another
- the correction of errors that have been discovered in the double-entry system

The use of the journal is necessary because:
- some transactions do not fit comfortably into one of the other subsidiary books
- even unusual transactions must first be entered into a subsidiary book
- it reduces the likelihood of only using one entry in the double-entry system
- as a part of the audit trail, it reduces the likelihood of fraud being perpetrated

There are a variety of source documents used to write up the journal, but the usual ones given in AS examination questions are invoices.

The layout of entries in the journal is important and is unique to the book. An entry in the journal looks like this:

	Dr £	Cr £
Motor vehicles	27 500	
Abcon Motors Ltd		27 500
Purchase of van BC 08 DEF from Abcon Motors Ltd		

The **sales day book** is a list of all the credit sales made to customers. Postings are made from the sales day book to the debit of each individual customer's account in the sales ledger. A credit entry is made (by using the total of all the debits entered in the sales ledger) in the sales account in the general ledger. (Remember that the sales day book is not part of the double-entry system.) It is written up from copy sales invoices; the copy is generally sent to the customer.

The **sales returns day book** is a list of goods returned by customers. The returns are posted individually to the credit of the customer's account in the sales ledger. A debit entry is made by using the total of all the credits entered in the sales ledger in the sales returns account (returns inwards) in the general ledger. It is written up from the copy credit note sent to the customer.

Do not enter the sales returns in the sales account. This results in a net sales figure and could mask an 'unacceptable' level of returns from customers.

The **purchases day book** is a list of purchases made on credit. Individual purchases are credited to the appropriate supplier's account in the purchases ledger. The debit entry in the purchases account in the general ledger is the total of the individual purchases listed.

The **purchase returns day book** lists goods returned to suppliers. Entries are made on the debit side of individual supplier's accounts in the general ledger. The credit entry in the purchase returns account is made up of the total of all the entries in the purchase returns day book. It is written up from credit notes received from the supplier.

The **cash book** is the subsidiary book in which all cash and bank transactions are recorded.

You should be able to record the information given on any source document in the correct subsidiary book. This is examined frequently, generally as part of a larger question involving double-entry transactions.

Double entry

It is essential that you master the basic concept of double entry. The key is to always remember that every transaction is entered twice in the ledger: one entry on the debit side of an account and one entry on the credit side of another account. In businesses that have many credit transactions, the ledger is generally split into three parts:

- **the sales ledger** — this contains the accounts of all customers the business deals with on credit terms.
- **the purchases ledger** — this contains the accounts of all the suppliers the business deals with on credit terms.
- **the general ledger** — this contains all other accounts.

The general rule is that a person's account (or other business's account) is contained in either the sales or purchases ledger, since the business's dealings with people (or other businesses) are as either a supplier or a customer.

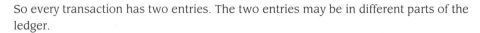

So every transaction has two entries. The two entries may be in different parts of the ledger.

Example:

Tony purchases goods for £236 for resale on credit from customers.

Prepare the appropriate accounts in Tony's ledger.

Answer:

	Purchases ledger			General ledger	
Dr	**Catherine**	**Cr**	**Dr**	**Purchases**	**Cr**
	Purchases	236	Catherine	236	

If you are asked in a question to prepare the accounts you must provide all the details. (You may use 'T' accounts when doing workings to help you answer a question.)

Here is an example taken from a general ledger:

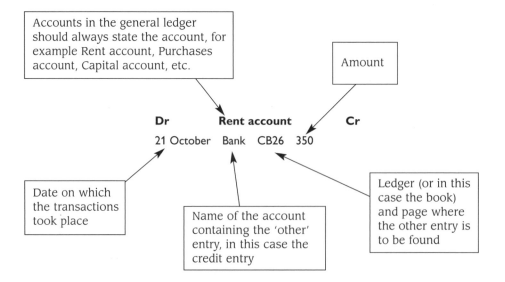

The details help to locate the other entry that completes the double entry. These 'locating devices' help if there is an error in any of the ledgers; they provide an audit trail.

Remember that all entries in the ledger must start their journey through the double-entry system in one of the subsidiary books.

If there is a balance on any account, always carry it down to start the next time period. If you do not, then you will forfeit a mark. The exception to this rule is when a question tells you specifically not to carry balances down.

Verification of accounting records

The trial balance

You should be able to prepare a trial balance almost as quickly as you are able to write down the details of each account summarised in the trial balance.

The trial balance is extracted from all the detailed accounts in the ledger(s). It is extracted on one day (usually the final day of the financial year) and so the heading tells us this.

Example: **Mary Marshall. Trial balance at 31 March 2008**

On the debit side of a trial balance you should only include assets and expenses. Examples include:

Assets	**Expenses**
Machinery	Rent
Vehicles	Motor expenses

On the credit side of a trial balance you should only include liabilities and incomes/benefits. Examples include:

Liabilities	**Incomes/benefits**
Mortgage	Sales
Bank loan	Discounts received
Capital	Rent received

It is helpful to remember this by using a mnemonic. (e.g. DRASEX — Dr Assets Expenses; CLIB — Cr Liabilities Incomes/benefits).

There are a few exceptions to the assets/expenses and liabilities/incomes or benefits rule — for example returns and drawings.

Returns inwards (goods previously sold but now returned by a customer, i.e. sales returns) will be on the opposite side of the trial balance to sales. Sales are a credit entry so sales returns must be a debit entry in the account and in the trial balance.

Returns outwards (goods previously purchased but now returned to the supplier, i.e. purchase returns) will be on the opposite side of the trial balance to purchases. Purchases are a debit entry so purchases returns must be a credit entry in the account and in the trial balance.

Drawings by the proprietor cause money to go out of a business and should be treated in the trial balance like other transactions that remove money from the business (i.e. expenses). Although the drawings are not a business expense, they are debited in the trial balance.

The trial balance is a summary of all the accounts in all the ledgers. So, an insurance account may look like this:

Dr			Insurance	Cr
8 January	Bank	127		
13 July	Bank	1386		
2 September	Bank	272		
9 November	Bank	931		

The trial balance would summarise the account and show:

Trial balance at 31 December 2008

	Dr	Cr
Insurance	2716	

The amount shown in the trial balance for trade debtors is the total of all the debit balances extracted from the sales ledger. Clearly, to list each individual balance from each account in the sales ledger on the trial balance for a business with many credit customers would result in a trial balance that might have to be written on a sheet of paper as long as a roll of wallpaper. Similarly, to list each trade creditor's balance could also result in a long list.

Why do people prepare a trial balance? The sole function of extracting a trial balance is to check the arithmetic accuracy of all the entries made in the ledgers. Additionally:

- The trial balance can disclose some errors in the double-entry system before the final accounts are prepared. If a trial balance does not balance, the final accounts cannot balance unless there are one or more compensating errors that counteract the discrepancy on the trial balance.
- Using the figures shown in the trial balance is easier than referring back to each individual account in the ledgers.
- It can help to prevent fraud if the ledgers are maintained by someone other than the person responsible for extracting the trial balance.

You must know the six types of error that are *not* revealed by extracting a trial balance that balances. You must also be able to describe an example of each type of error. Learn a mnemonic such as CROPOC. The six types of error are:

(1) **Commission** — an entry is made in an incorrect account of a similar type. For example, a motor vehicles account is debited with an entry that should have been debited to office equipment or the account of Thomas and Son is credited with credit purchases received from Thompson.

(2) **Reversal** — a debit entry and credit entry is made which should in fact have been a credit entry and a debit entry. For example, goods for resale purchased on credit from Mansoor is debited to Mansoor and credited to the purchases account.

(3) **Omission** — neither a debit nor a credit entry is made; there has been no record made in the double-entry system. For example, a purchase invoice has been lost, so no entry is made in the purchase day book. As a result, no entry is made in a

personal account in the purchases ledger and no entry is made in the purchases account in the general ledger.

(4) Principle — entries are debited or credited in the wrong class of account. This type of error makes the profit and loss account and the balance sheet incorrect. For example, a van purchased for use in the business is debited to the motor expenses account.

(5) Original entry — an error is made when entering the information from a source document to one of the subsidiary books. For example, goods valued at £123 sold to a credit customer is entered in the sales day book as £132.

(6) Compensating error — error(s) on the debit side of an account(s) equals error(s) on the credit side of an account(s).

Suspense accounts

When a trial balance fails to balance, the difference is placed in a temporary account called a **suspense account**. If the debit side of a trial balance is larger than the credit side, insert a 'suspense' item on the credit side so that the debit and credit columns have the same total. If the credit side of a trial balance is larger than the debit side, insert a 'suspense' item on the debit side so that the debit and credit columns have the same total. When you have corrected the errors given in a question, the suspense item is cancelled out and the trial balance will balance.

Some exam questions do not give the original trial balance difference. You may have to calculate this by entering errors in a suspense account. The figures used in the suspense account will mean that it does not balance. The 'missing figure' is the amount by which the trial balance did not balance before the errors were corrected.

Remember that the trial balance is a summary of all the balances extracted from all of the ledgers. So if you have to add an extra debit in your suspense account to make it balance, this means that there was a missing debit balance, i.e. suspense account debit balance on the trial balance before the errors were discovered.

You must be able to adjust gross profit and net profit figures to take into account any errors corrected. Errors requiring adjustments to:

- sales
- purchases
- sales returns
- purchases returns
- carriage inwards

affect gross profit and net profit figures calculated before the errors were corrected.

Errors requiring adjustments to:

- expenses
- incomes/benefits (discount received, rent received, etc.)

affect net profit only.

Errors requiring adjustments to:
- assets
- liabilities

do not affect gross profit or net profit *unless* the error is an error of principle, such as a new motor van (£36 000) being included as motor expenses. Correction of this error of principle would cause profits to rise by £36 000.

Bank reconciliation statements

This is a popular topic with examiners. It is less popular with candidates.

When a business has a current account with a bank, the owners of that business keep a record of dealings using the bank account. The bank also keeps a record of the same transactions in its ledger. The bank sends a copy of its record in the form of a bank statement at intervals agreed with the customer. When a bank statement is received from a bank, a trader compares this copy of the bank's records with his/her own records shown in the bank columns of his/her cash book.

The purpose of preparing a bank reconciliation statement is to check the accuracy of the entries in the bank columns of the cash book by using an independently prepared document (the bank statement). The two balances should agree because they are both prepared using the same amounts. However, the balance shown in a trader's cash book (bank columns) may not agree with the balance shown on the bank statement on the same date (see below).

Remember that a debit bank balance given in a trader's cash book shows that a trader has money in the bank, and a credit balance means that the business has an overdraft. However, because a bank statement is a copy of the bank's records, the opposite is true. A debit balance on a bank statement means the account is overdrawn and a credit balance shows that the business has money in the bank account.

Remember that the cash book balance is the one that is used in the trial balance and in the business balance sheet.

You should know and remember the reasons why the two balances might not agree.

Possible cash book balance errors

The balance in a trader's books of accounts may not agree with the balance in the bank's records for two reasons:
(1) Time differences in recording transactions:
  - When a trader lodges money in the bank, the transaction is recorded immediately in the trader's cash book using the paying-in slip counterfoil as the source document. The bank may not credit the trader's account until a couple of days later.
  - When a trader writes out a cheque, it is recorded immediately in the trader's

cash book using the cheque counterfoil as the source document. The bank does not credit the account until the cheque is presented for payment.

(2) Lack of knowledge by the trader:
- The bank debits a trader's account with bank charges, interest etc., but the trader remains unaware of the amounts until the appropriate bank statement is received.
- The bank may credit a trader's account with counter credits or payments made directly into the account without the trader's knowledge. The trader may be unaware of the amounts until either a bank statement or notification is received.
- The bank may dishonour a cheque. The trader would be unaware of this until a bank statement or notification is received.

General errors

It is now rare for banks to make the following errors. The major error made by banks is to debit or credit an amount that should be entered in another business account. Nevertheless, you should be aware of the possibility of:
- casting errors in the cash book
- entering incorrect amounts in the cash book
- entering items on the wrong side of the cash book

Procedure used to answer a question

In order to answer an examination question, you are generally required to prepare two elements:
- You must update the cash book since this is part of the business records.
- You must then prepare the actual reconciliation statement.

A good procedure to follow is:

(1) Balance the bank columns of the cash book and carry the balance down.

(2) Compare the bank columns of the cash book with the entries shown on the bank statement.

(3) Bring the cash book up to date by:
   (a) entering payments shown as paid by the bank that have not been entered in the credit bank column of the cash book
   (b) entering any amounts received by the bank that have not been entered in the debit bank column of the cash book.

(4) Correct any errors discovered in the bank columns of the cash book. (Remember that, when comparing the cash book entries with the bank statement entries, the bank statement entries are always assumed to be correct.)

(5) If the bank statement contains errors, inform the bank and ask for an adjusted bank statement balance.

(6) Prepare the bank reconciliation statement.

Learn the layout of a bank reconciliation statement and always use a heading. An example is given on p. 20:

T. Relph. Bank reconciliation statement at 30 June 2008

	£	£
Balance at bank as per cash book		582
Add unpresented cheques		
cheque number 137	42	
cheque number 151	28	
cheque number 165	37	
		107
		689
Less lodgements not yet credited		416
Balance at bank as per bank statement		273

If there is more than one unpresented cheque then it is safer to list these in the reconciliation statement. If you add them on your calculator and you make an error the examiner cannot award any part marks.

Sales and purchases ledger control accounts

Control accounts only verify the arithmetic accuracy of the entries in the ledger being checked. There could be errors in the control account that remain undetected. These are errors of:

- commission
- reversal
- omission
- original entry
- compensating errors

These errors are the same as those detailed in the errors not affecting the balancing of a trial balance (see pp. 16–17). You must learn them.

The type of error missing is errors of principle. Why would an error of principle not be revealed when you prepare a ledger control account? Answer: an error of principle would be an entry in the wrong class of account in the general ledger. Neither entry would, generally, be entered in a personal ledger.

Set-offs or contra items

A business may be both a supplier and customer to another business. For example, Ash & Co sells timber valued at £1200 on credit to C. Hair, a furniture manufacturer. Ash purchases four office desks on credit for £800 from Hair. The entries in the ledgers of Ash would show:

	Purchases ledger page 42				Sales ledger page 61	
Dr	Hair	Cr	Dr	Hair		Cr
	Office equipment	800	Sales	1200		

Note that the descriptions tell us where the opposite entry is to be located. There is a debit entry of £800 in the office equipment account in the general ledger. There is a credit entry of £1200 in the sales account in the general ledger.

It would not be sensible for Ash to demand £1200 payment from Hair and to send Hair a cheque for £800. As the amount due to Ash is greater than the amount owed by Ash, it would seem sensible to set off the amount owed to Ash against the amount owed by Ash.

	Purchases ledger			Sales ledger	
Dr	Hair	Cr	Dr	Hair	Cr
Transfer to sales ledger 800			Transfer from purchases ledger		800

This transaction would be recorded in the journal as the appropriate subsidiary book.

Transfer of credit balance in Hair's account in the purchases ledger to Hair's account in the sales ledger:

Journal			
Hair	PL 42	800	
Hair	SL 61		800

After this transfer, the ledgers would show:

	Purchases ledger page 42			
Dr	Hair			Cr
Transfer to sales ledger	800	Office equipment		800

	Sales ledger page 61			
Dr	Hair			Cr
Sales	1200	Transfer from purchases ledger		800

All entries in any personal ledger must also show in a control account. There are:
- a debit entry for £800 in Ash's purchases ledger control account
- a credit entry for £800 in Ash's sales ledger control account

Schedules of debtors and creditors

These are lists of balances extracted from the sales and purchases ledgers:
- **schedule of debtors** — a list of all the debit balances extracted from the sales ledger
- **schedule of creditors** — a list of all the credit balances extracted from the purchases ledger

Credit balances in the sales ledger must not be netted out with the debit balances. Debit balances in the purchases ledger must not be netted out with the credit balances.

The total of the schedule debtors should equal the debit balance shown in the sales ledger control account. The total of the schedule of creditors should equal the credit balances shown in the purchases ledger control account.

Preparing a control account

In a business that has a large number of credit customers and credit suppliers, there will be many entries made in the sales ledger and purchases ledger. This means that there is great potential for errors to be made. Control accounts are used to check the accuracy of the entries made in each of the sales ledgers and each of the purchases ledgers.

A control account is a summary of all the entries that have been made in each sales ledger and each purchases ledger in any particular month. Any entry in any sales ledger or purchases ledger is duplicated in the appropriate control account. Some businesses maintain control accounts as part of their double-entry system, while others maintain the control accounts as memorandum accounts. For the purposes of the examination, there is no difference in their preparation.

Practise preparing individual accounts as they would appear in the appropriate ledger. If you can do this then you should be able to prepare the control account for that ledger — they are similar and only the magnitude of the figures will be different.

Examples:

Sales ledger					Sales ledger control account			
Dr		**B. Keaton**		**Cr**	**Dr**			**Cr**
Balance b/d	123	Returns inward	57		Balance b/d	123 000	Returns inward	57 000
Sales	217	Cash	200		Sales	217 000	Cash	200 000
		Discount all'd	22				Discount all'd	22 000
		Balance c/d	61				Balance c/d	61 000
	340		340			340 000		340 000
Balance b/d	61				Balance b/d	61 000		

Follow the same principles when preparing a purchases ledger control account.

Remember that if an entry in the double-entry system does not appear in a personal ledger then it will not appear in a control account.

You should know where each of the figures used in a control account comes from. They all come from a total extracted from a subsidiary book. In the example above of a sales ledger control account:

- sales £217 000 is the total of the credit sales recorded in the sales day book
- returns inward £57 000 is the total of the goods returned recorded in the sales returns day book.
- cash £200 000 is the total of cash received from customers recorded in the cash book
- discount allowed £22 000 is the total of the discount allowed columns in the cash book

Trading and profit and loss accounts and balance sheets

Trading and profit and loss accounts

You must be able to prepare trading accounts and profit and loss accounts quickly and above all accurately from a trial balance, taking into account any additional information given in the question. To speed up your preparations of these accounts, practise marking alongside each item given in a trial balance: 'T' for trading account, 'P' for profit and loss account, and 'B' for balance sheet. This can help when you start your answer. In most, if not all, examinations you will find a question that requires the preparation of:

- a trading account, or
- a profit and loss account, or
- a combined trading and profit and loss account

You must practise the layout used by your teacher and in textbooks. Good layouts could be rewarded with a quality of presentation mark (or two).

Some items in trading accounts that cause students problems include the following.

Headings

Always use a full heading. Do not abbreviate any part of the heading. The heading should include the business name. An example might be:

R. Rajan. Trading account for the year ended 31 March 2009

Note that there are no abbreviations (except for the first name) in the title or the date.

Returns

Inset returns and extend the net sales and net purchases into the main body of your answer. For example:

A. Smith. Trading account for the year ended 30 April 2009

	£	£	£
Sales		210 367	
Less returns inwards		1 248	209 119
Less cost of sales			
Stock 1 May 2008		15 762	
Purchases	96 499		
Less returns outwards	634	95 865	
		111 627	
Stock 30 April 2009		17 498	94 129
Gross profit			114 990

Note that 'gross profit' is written in full — abbreviating the words will cost you a mark — and that the cost of sales is identified.

Some people prefer to identify the cost of sales figure in the line above the gross profit.

A. Smith. Trading account for the year ended 30 April 2009

	£	£	£
Sales			210 367
Less returns inwards			1 248
			209 119
Stock 1 May 2008		15 762	
Purchases	96 499		
Less returns outwards	634	95 865	
		111 627	
Stock 30 April 2009		17 498	
Cost of sales			94 129
Gross profit			114 990

This is equally acceptable as a layout. Choose the one you feel most comfortable using and use it always.

Goods taken out of the business

Goods taken out of the business for the use of the proprietor should not be included in the final accounts of the business so they are deducted from purchases. They must also be included as part of the owner's drawings. Show your calculation as workings.

For example:

R. Roy. Trading account for the year ended 28 February 2009

	£	£
Sales		72 488
Less cost of sales		
Stock 1 March 2008	748	
Purchases	26 103	
	26 851	
Stock 28 February 2009	649	26 202
Gross profit		46 286

27 603 purchases less 1500 goods for own use

Carriage

Carriage inwards is shown as an addition to purchases since carriage inwards makes the purchases more expensive. For example:

P. Lefevre. Trading account for the year ended 31 March 2009

	£	£	£
Sales			143 003
Less cost of sales			
Stock 1 April 2008		7 461	
Purchases	64 728		
Carriage inwards	643	65 371	
		72 832	
Stock 31 March 2009		8 112	64 720
Gross profit			78 283

Carriage outwards is an expense that is shown in the profit and loss account.

The profit and loss account must also have a full heading. An example is:

A. Lim. Profit and loss account for the year ended 31 January 2009

Note that there are no abbreviations in the title or the date.

Other items in a profit and loss account can cause problems to some students.

Accruals

The value of resources that are used to produce sales (and consequently profits) must be accounted for in the financial year of use, whether or not they have been paid for.

For example, wages amounting to £37 430 have been paid during the financial year (amount shown on trial balance). At the year end, wages amounting to £674 remain unpaid. £674 of workers' skills and expertise, although used during the financial year, have not yet been paid for by the business. This amount needs to be added to £37 430 to give the total use of resources during the year. The amount entered under expenses in the profit and loss account for wages is £38 104 (£37 430 + £674).

Prepayments

We are only interested in expenditure for the financial year in question. That is what our heading tells us: 'Profit and loss account for the year...'. Any amounts paid for the next financial year must be disregarded.

For example, insurances amounting to £1794 have been paid during the financial year (amount shown on the trial balance). At the year end, insurances paid in advance (i.e. for the following financial year) amounted to £287. £287 has been paid for insurance for the following financial year and should be included in next year's profit and loss account as an expense. Only £1507 (£1794 – £287) should be shown in this year's final accounts.

Although you may have adjusted for accruals and/or prepayments dozens of times in class and when doing your homework, do the calculation carefully — and although you probably do the calculation on your calculator, write down (as workings) exactly what you have done. If you make an error, you will probably then score part marks.

Discounts

Discounts received increase net profit and so are added to the gross profit. Discount allowed is regarded as an expense. Although it is acceptable to net the cash discounts and use only one figure in the profit and loss account instead of two, it is safer to show the two discounts separately. (You could make an error deducting one from the other.)

Provision for depreciation of fixed assets

The value of any resources used to generate sales (and consequently profits) must be accounted for in the financial year of use. When a fixed asset is used to generate profits then a proportion of the cost of the asset is shown as an expense in the profit and loss account. Only the change in the provision is shown in the profit and loss account. For example:

Provision for depreciation of office equipment at 31 December 2008   £16 000
Provision for depreciation of office equipment at 31 December 2009   £20 000

The profit and loss account for the year ended 31 December 2009 would show, under expenses, provision for depreciation of office equipment as £4000.

The provision at the start of the year will be shown in the trial balance. The provision at the end of the year will need to be calculated. For example:

- Provision for depreciation of vehicles at 30 November 2007 (shown on trial balance): £24 000. Provision for depreciation of vehicles is calculated using the straight-line method at 20% per annum.
- Vehicles at cost at 30 November 2008: £125 000.
- Provision for depreciation of vehicles at 30 November 2008: 20% × £125 000 = £25 000
- The amount to be shown as an expense in the profit and loss account for the year ended 30 November 2008 is £1000 (£25 000 − £24 000).

Examiners can make the calculation more difficult by including the purchase of further assets during the financial year. For example:
- Provision for depreciation of machinery at 31 March 2008 (shown on trial balance): £18 000.
- Provision for depreciation of machinery is calculated using the straight-line method at 10% of machinery held at the year end.
- Machinery at cost at 31 March 2007: £45 000.
- During October 2007 a new machine costing £17 000 was purchased.
- Provision for depreciation of machinery at 31 March 2009: £24 200.
- The amount shown as an expense in the profit and loss account for the year ended 31 March 2009 is £6200 [(£45 000 + £17 000) × 10%].

Balance sheets

You must be able to prepare a balance sheet in good form, quickly and accurately from a trial balance, taking into account any additional information given in the question. Make sure that you are able to classify assets into fixed assets and current assets and liabilities into long-term liabilities and current liabilities. Label the headings clearly and do not use abbreviations.
- Fixed assets are used to yield benefits for the business for more than 1 year.
- Current assets are cash or assets that are changed into cash within 1 year.
- Long-term liabilities are debts owed by a business that are repaid in more than 1 year's time.
- Current liabilities are debts owed by a business that need to be repaid within 1 year.

Capital is the term used to describe how much a business is worth to the proprietor. It is also the amount of money that the owner has invested in the business. It is made up of the money that the owner has injected into the business, plus any profits reinvested over the business's lifetime, less any withdrawals of cash or goods (drawings) made over the years of ownership.

You must also be able to close down the nominal accounts shown in a general ledger. In addition, you must be able to incorporate into these accounts any accruals and prepayments that may be outstanding at the end of the financial year.

Example:

The following rent account appears in the general ledger of a business at 31 December 2008.

Rent account

Dr				**Cr**
3 January	Bank	CB28		300
28 April	Bank	CB47		300
17 August	Bank	CB68		300

The payment due on 1 October 2008 had not been paid at the financial year end, 31 December 2008. Rent is due quarterly on 1 January, 1 April, 1 July and 1 October.

Prepare the rent account as it would appear at the financial year end.

Answer:

At the year end £300 rent is owing. The safest way to prepare the account is to follow this procedure.

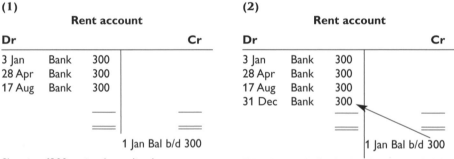

(1)

Rent account

Dr				**Cr**
3 Jan	Bank	300		
28 Apr	Bank	300		
17 Aug	Bank	300		

1 Jan Bal b/d 300

Showing £300 owing (a creditor)

(2)

Rent account

Dr				**Cr**
3 Jan	Bank	300		
28 Apr	Bank	300		
17 Aug	Bank	300		
31 Dec	Bank	300		

1 Jan Bal b/d 300

Take the credit 'back into the account' thus completing the double entry. A credit requires a corresponding debit.

(3) Add the 'heaviest' side and balance the account with a transfer to the profit and loss account.

Rent account

Dr				**Cr**	
3 January	Bank	300			
28 April	Bank	300			
17 August	Bank	300			
31 December	Balance c/d	300	31 December Profit and loss account	1200	
		1200		1200	
			1 January Balance b/d	300	

So, rent £1200 appears as an expense in the profit and loss account for the year. The credit balance £300 appears on the balance sheet as a current liability.

A similar process is followed to record any prepayments in the general ledger.

Example:

At the financial year ended 31 December 2008, £150 has been paid for business rates due in the financial year ended 31 December 2009.

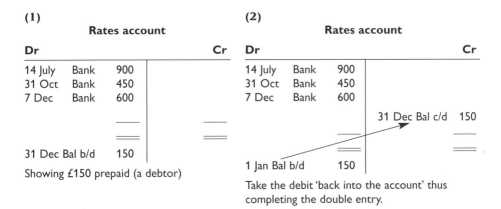

(1)

Rates account

Dr			Cr
14 July	Bank	900	
31 Oct	Bank	450	
7 Dec	Bank	600	
31 Dec Bal b/d	150		

Showing £150 prepaid (a debtor)

(2)

Rates account

Dr			Cr
14 July	Bank	900	
31 Oct	Bank	450	
7 Dec	Bank	600	
			31 Dec Bal c/d 150
1 Jan Bal b/d	150		

Take the debit 'back into the account' thus completing the double entry.

(3) Add the 'heaviest' side and balance the account with a transfer to the profit and loss account.

Rates account

Dr			Cr	
14 July	Bank	900		
31 October	Bank	450	31 December Profit and loss account	1800
7 December	Bank	600	31 December Balance c/d	150
		1950		1950
1 January Balance b/d	150			

Remember that the term 'debit balance' refers to the balance on the account at the start of the new accounting period and that the term 'credit balance' refers to the balance on the account at the start of the new accounting period. The safest way to ensure that you do not make an error is to always write in any balance 'underneath' the account and then transfer the same amount diagonally up into the account.

Also remember that the balances remaining on any account at the end of a financial year need to be shown on the balance sheet at the end of an accounting period.

Bad debts

A bad debt occurs when a debtor cannot pay the amount that is owed. If it is known that a debtor cannot settle his/her account, then it would be inappropriate to leave a debit balance in the account since a debit balance on an account represents an asset. If the balance was left on the account:
• the total amount owed by debtors would be overstated

- the total amount of current assets shown on the balance sheet would be overstated
- the total amount of all assets shown on the balance sheet would be overstated
- the capital shown on the balance sheet would be overstated

When it is certain that a debtor cannot settle the outstanding debt, the debit balance on the account cannot be allowed to remain for the reasons listed above. The debt must be written off:

- The bad debts account in the general ledger is debited.
- The customer's account in the sales ledger is credited.

The bad debts account is closed at the end of the financial year by transferring the total to the profit and loss account thus:

Bad debts account

Dr			Cr
Arthur Baines	179	Profit and loss account	809
Carol Dixon	83		
Gahir Jasdeep	135		
Elly Forsyth	412		
	809		809

In this unit you will not have to prepare the bad debts account, but the entries above show the process involved.

Questions
&
Answers

This section contains ten questions, each dealing with different topics in the unit. Each question is followed by two sample answers interspersed with comments from the examiner.

The questions are typical of those you could be faced with in your AS examination. They are based on the format of the AS examination papers. The usual pattern is that the first part of the question tests your ability to solve a numerical problem using knowledge, understanding and application skills. The second part of the question generally involves some analysis and then an evaluation of a scenario.

Sample answers

In each case, the first answer (by candidate A) is intended to show the type of response that would earn a grade A. Remember that a grade-A response does not mean that the answer is perfect. You will see that there is a range of marks that could score a grade A.

The answers given by candidate B illustrate the types of error that many weaker candidates tend to make and so deprive themselves of vital marks that could so easily have moved their script up a grade.

Resist the temptation to look at the answers before or during the answering of the question.

Examiner comments

The examiner comments are preceded by the icon 🄴. In some cases they are shown within the candidate's answer, but in the main they appear after the candidate's answer. In weaker answers, the comments point out areas for improvement and the types of common error found in answers that are around the pass/fail boundary.

Question 1

Source documents and subsidiary books

Complete the table below to show the subsidiary book in which the source document is entered and the accounts to be debited and credited. The first one has been done for you.

	Source document	Subsidiary book	Debit entry	Credit entry
1 Purchase of goods for resale	Purchases invoice	Purchases day book	Purchases	Supplier's account
2 Discount allowed to a credit customer				
3 Bank charges				
4 Unsuitable goods returned by credit customer				
5 Transfer of debit balance on Barker's account in sales ledger to Barker's account in the purchase ledger				
6 Goods paid for by cheque				
7 Invoice for the purchase of office equipment on credit				

(24 marks)

■ ■ ■

Answer to question 1: candidate A

2 Cash book ✗	Cash book ✓	Discount allowed ✓	Cash book ✗
3 Bank statement ✓	Cash book ✓	Bank charges ✓	Bank account ✓
4 Credit note ✓	Sales Ret. DB ✓	Sales returns ✓	Customer account ✓
5 Invoice ✗	Journal ✓	Barker Sales ledger ✗	Barker Sales ledger ✓
6 Cheque stub ✓	Cash book ✓	Supplier's account ✓	Bank account ✓
7 Invoice ✓	Journal ✓	Office equipment ✓	Supplier's account ✓

🖉 This is a good answer. The candidate succeeds in 20 out of the 24 responses.

2) This part is rather tricky. The discount allowed would be offered on the sales invoice and so the response should be copy sales invoice. The discount columns in the cash book are memorandum columns — i.e. they are not part of the double-entry system — they help to collect all the discount entries. The discount allowed account is debited and the customer's account is credited.

5) This part is also difficult. The transfer would be noted in a memorandum, probably instigated by the ledger clerk or by a credit controller. The account to be debited would be Barker's account in the purchases ledger. The candidate seems to have

hedged his/her bets in this case, by giving the same answer for the debit entry and the credit entry. Alternative answers could have been debit purchases ledger control account and credit sales ledger control.

The candidate scores 20 out of 24 marks — a grade A.

■ ■ ■

Answer to question 1: candidate B

2 Cash book ✗	Cash book ✓	Cash book ✗	Cash book ✗
3 Bank statement ✓	Cash book ✓	Bank charges ✓	Cash book ✓
4 Credit note ✓	Returns day book ✗	Sales returns ✓	Sales ✗
5 Invoices ✗	Sales day book and purchases day book ✗	Sales ledger ✗	Purchases ledger ✗
6 Cheque book stub ✓	Cash book ✓	Supplier ✓	Cash book ✓
7 Journal ✗	Purchases day book ✗	Office equipment ✓	Fixed asset account ✗

2) The candidate knows that the discount allowed column appears in the cash book but does not realise that the double entry should debit the discount allowed account in the general ledger and credit the supplier's account.

3) Although bank charges appear on the bank statement, this is not part of the records kept by a business. The bank statement is a copy of the records kept by a business. The bank statement is a copy of the bank's records sent to a customer of the bank.

4) Returns day book is not precise enough. The candidate should identify the day book. He/she clearly knows that the credit note has been sent to the customer to record sales returns. Crediting sales would seem to indicate a further sale to the customer.

5) This is a difficult part of the question. One of the uses to which the journal is put is to record inter-ledger transfers. The two accounts are reversed. The candidate ought to have cleared the debit balance on Barker's account in the sales ledger with a credit balance and then completed the double entry with a debit balance in Barker's account in the purchases ledger.

7) The purchases day book is reserved for purchases of goods for resale. However, the candidate could have scored a mark had he/she stated 'Analysed purchases day book'.

The candidate scores 12 out of 24 marks — a grade E.

Subsidiary books and ledger accounts

The accounts in the ledgers of C. Faraz, a trader, at 1 March 2009 show the following balances:

	£
Purchases	30 142
Sales	92 460
Carriage inwards	933
Returns inwards	2 163
Returns outwards	701
Stock	2 968
Rent	4 400

The subsidiary books for March 2009 show:

	£
Sales day book	9 786
Purchases day book	3 466
Sales returns day book	820
Purchases returns day book	477

The journal has the following entry:

	Dr	Cr
	£	£
Returns inwards		86
Carriage inwards	86	

Additional information
(1) Carriage inward entered in error as returns inwards.
(2) Rent remaining unpaid at 31 March 2009 was £400.
(3) Stock at 31 March 2009 was £3420.

REQUIRED

(a) Enter the balances in the appropriate ledger accounts at 1 March 2009. (7 marks)

(b) Make entries in the ledger accounts to record the information given for March 2009. (8 marks)

(c) Make entries in the ledger accounts necessary to prepare a trading and profit and loss account for the year ended 31 March 2009. (7 marks)

(d) Prepare a trading account for the year ended 31 March 2009. (9 marks)

■ ■ ■

Answer to question 2: candidate A

Purchases account

Bal b/d	30 142	Trading a/c	33 608
PDB	3 466		
	33 608		33 608

Sales account

Trading a/c	102 246	Bal b/d	92 460
		SDB	9 786
	102 246		102 246

Carriage inwards

Bal b/d	933	Trading a/c	933

Returns inwards

Bal b/d	2163	Trading a/c	2983
SRDB	820		
	2983		2983

Returns outwards

		Balance b/d	701
Trading a/c	1178	PRDB	477
	1178		1178

Stock

Closing stock	3420	Opening stock	2968

Rent

Bal b/d	4400	P & L a/c	4800
Bal c/d	400		
	4800		4800
		Bal b/d	400

🄔 This is an important question testing knowledge, understanding and application skills in a number of key areas. It has to be tackled with a systematic approach.

The candidate scores 17 marks: 6/7 for (a), 5/8 for (b) and 6/7 for (c). The stock account proves to be difficult for this candidate. The closing balance is entered correctly, but the opening balance should be entered as a debit and written off to the trading account. The inter-account transfer from the journal has not been attempted. The other accounts are completed accurately.

(d)

C. Faraz. Trading account for the year ended 31 March 2009

	£	£	£
Sales			102 246
Returns inwards			2 983
			99 263
Less cost of sales			
Stock		2 968	
Purchases	33 608		
Carriage inwards	933		
	34 541		
Returns outward	1 178	33 363	
		36 331	
Stock		3 420	32 911
Gross profit			66 352

This is a perfect answer that scores 9 marks. It is well laid out and accurate, using the candidate's own figures from part (b). The candidate has included the heading without abbreviations and the gross profit has been identified clearly.

The candidate scores 26 out of 31 marks — an A-grade answer.

■ ■ ■

Answer to question 2: candidate B

Purchases

Bal b/d	30 142		
PDB	3 466	P & L a/c	33 608

Sales

		Bal b/d	92 460
P & L a/c	102 246	SDB	9 786

Carriage inward

Bal b/d	933	CI	86
		P & L a/c	847

Returns inwards

Bal b/d	2163	CI	86
		P & L a/c	2077

Returns outwards

PRDB	477	Bal b/d	701
P & L a/c	224		

Stock

Rent

		Bal b/d	4400
Bal c/d	4800	Bal c/d	400

The purchases and sales accounts are prepared accurately. Both returns accounts contain errors, but are rewarded as 'own figures' in the trading account. Although the description 'P & L a/c' is incorrect (it should be 'trading account'), the candidate is given the benefit of the doubt. The inter-account transfer from the journal shows two credit entries — only the entry in the returns inwards account scores. The rent account is reversed and the balance is not brought down. Remember that every debit needs a credit to complete the picture and that balances must always be brought down (unless the question tells you not to); otherwise you will always drop a mark. Overall, the candidate scores 12 marks: 5/7 for (a), 3/8 for (b) and 4/7 for (c).

(d)

C. Faraz. P & L account y/e 31/3/09

	£	£	£
Sales			102 246
Returns inwards			2 077
			100 169
Less cost of sales			
Stock		2 968	
Purchases	33 608		
Carriage inward	847		
	32 761		
Returns outward	224	32 985	
		35 953	
Stock		3 240	32 713
GP			67 456

 Here 4 marks are scored for sales, sales returns, opening stock and purchases. The heading has too many abbreviations to gain the presentation mark — there should be no abbreviations. The description for gross profit has also been abbreviated. Carriage outwards is deducted and returns outwards are added.

 Overall, this candidate earns 16 marks out 31, which is not good enough for a pass grade.

Trading and profit and loss accounts and balance sheets

The following balances have been extracted from the books of account of Linda Leigh *after* the preparation of a trading account.

Balances at 31 December 2008

	£
Bank loan repayable 2019	15 000
Bank overdraft	1 369
Capital	47 824
Drawings	21 300
Equipment — at cost	72 000
— depreciation	27 000
General expenses	21 326
Gross profit	96 438
Motor expenses	8 612
Rent and rates	9 400
Stock at 31 December 2008	12 400
Telephone	9 920
Trade creditors	6 307
Trade debtors	9 472
Wages	56 116

Additional information at 31 December 2008
(1) Telephone rental £160 has been paid in advance.
(2) Wages owing amounted to £612.
(3) A schedule of debtors extracted from the sales ledger at 31 December 2008 shows:

	£
Bradbury	341
Mousaka	128
All other debtors	9003
	9472

The debts of Bradbury and Mousaka have been outstanding for well over 2 years and Linda has decided to write them off as bad.

REQUIRED

Prepare:
(a) the following accounts as they would appear after the preparation of a profit and loss account for the year ended 31 December 2008 (open each account with the balance shown in the list above)
  (i) Telephone account
  (ii) Wages account

(iii) Bradbury

(iv) Mousaka (12 marks)

(b) a profit and loss account for the year ended 31 December 2008 (10 marks)

plus 1 mark for presentation

(c) a balance sheet extract showing current assets *and* current liabilities (6 marks)

plus 1 mark for presentation

■ ■ ■

Answer to question 3: candidate A

(a)

Telephone account

31 December Trial balance	9920	31 December Profit & loss account	9760
		31 December Balance c/d	160
	9920		9920
1 January Balance b/d	160		

Wages account

31 December Trial balance	56 116	31 December Profit & loss account	56 728
31 December Balance c/d	612		
	56 728		56 728
		1 January Balance b/d	612

Bradbury account

31 December Bal b/d	341	31 December Bad debts a/c	341
	341		341

Mousaka account

31 December Bal b/d	128	31 December Bad debts	128
	128		128

✍ This is a good, clear account. Remember that if a question asks for accounts, they should contain as much detail as possible. Dates and descriptions are essential if you are to score maximum marks. Note that the candidate gives correct dates for the balances brought down, which start Linda's accounts off in the New Year. (It is highly unlikely that folio references will be given.) One minor detail: headings for accounts in the general ledger do have the word 'account' in them, but it is not usual to use 'account' in the headings in the sales and purchases ledgers. This answer earns 12 out of 12 marks.

(b)

Linda Leigh. Trading and profit and loss account for the year ended 31 December 2008

	£	£	
Gross profit		96 438	
Less expenses			
General expenses	21 326		
Motor expenses	8 612		
Rent and rates	9 400		
Telephone	9 760		*wkg 9920 – 160*
Wages	56 728		*wkg 56 116 + 612*
Bad debts	469		*wkg 341 + 128*
Depreciation	9 000	115 295	
Net ~~profit~~ loss		18 857	

This is a perfect profit and loss account and scores maximum marks. Two points worth noting are:

(1) The candidate provides workings (shown in italics) that are not absolutely necessary, since the working has been done in the accounts in part (a) of the answer. However, he/she may have felt safer using this approach.

(2) The candidate realises that his/her net profit is in fact a loss — the word 'profit' has been crossed out and the word 'loss' inserted. Do not alter figures or words: cross them out and write the new figure or word above or alongside. This will help both you and the examiner. The presentation mark is scored — the heading is perfect and the loss is described correctly.

(c)

Linda Leigh. Balance sheet extract at 31 December 2008

	£	£
Current assets		
Stock	12 400	
Trade debtors	9 003	
Prepayment – telephone	160	21 563
Current liabilities		
Trade creditors	6 307	
Bank overdraft	1 369	
Accrued expenses-wages	612	8 288
Working capital		13 285

 The question asks you to show current assets and current liabilities. This candidate does all this and scores maximum marks. He/she also shows the working capital figure, which is not asked for, so the casting error is not penalised (working capital should be £13 275). Do not give an examiner an answer or part of an answer that is not asked for. The presentation mark is scored for the balance sheet heading and the headings 'current assets' and 'current liabilities'. Notice also the use of the word 'extract' in the heading.

 The candidate earns 28 'accounting' marks plus 2 marks for presentation.

■ ■ ■

Answer to question 3: candidate B

(a)

£

Telephone

T B	9920	P & L a/c	9760
	____	Bal	160

Wages

TB	56 116	P & L a/c	56 728
Bal	612		____

Bradbury

Bal	341	Bad debt	341

Mousaka

bal	128	Bad debt	128

 The candidate shows a casual approach to answering this part of the question. However, the answer is worth 10 marks. He/she could have scored the other 2 marks by bringing down the accrual and prepayment balances. Remember to give all details in full. Once you get into this habit, it will become second nature to you and will ensure that you always score any presentation marks in a question.

(b)

L Lee. Trading and profit and loss account for the period ended 31 December 2008

	£	£
GP		96 438
Gen expenses	21 326	
Motor exp	8 612	
Rent	9 400	
Telephone	9 920	
Wages	56 116	
Depn	36 000	141 374
Nprofit		44 936

Only 4 marks are scored out of 11. The heading contains three errors: the name is incorrect; the candidate has not prepared a trading account; and the profit and loss account is for the year (a period could be 2 hours, 20 weeks, 15 years etc.). The presentation marks are lost through the use of many abbreviations. Do not throw away the presentation marks; they are easy to score, but they are easy to lose if you are careless.

The adjustments made in part (a) are not followed through into the profit and loss account; depreciation is calculated incorrectly and the loss is described as a profit.

(c)

Current assets

Stock	12 400
Drs	9 472
Wages	612

Current liabilities

Crs	6 307
Bank o/d	1 369
Telephone	160

This candidate scores 3 marks out of 7. Only stock, trade creditors and the bank overdraft are correct. The presentation mark is not gained: there is no balance sheet heading, although the current asset and current liabilities headings are written in full. The accruals and prepayments are carelessly classified incorrectly. Debtors are not adjusted to take into account the bad debts written off.

Overall, the candidate scores 17 marks out of 30 — only just a pass grade. With more care and more attention to detail the candidate could obtain a higher mark.

Question 4

The cash book

Carole Chung provides the following information for the week ended 31 October 2008. It has not been entered in her cash book.

24 October	Cash sales	528.65
25 October	Cheque received from Mitchel Ltd (discount allowed £29.78)	962.92
25 October	Cheque paid to Compo (discount received £5.60)	106.40
26 October	Cheque drawn for own private use	120.00
27 October	Rent paid by cash	80.00
27 October	Cash sales	745.88
28 October	Cash paid into bank	600.00
28 October	Dishonoured cheque returned by bank	73.87
30 October	Wages paid by cash	567.34
31 October	Overdraft interest charged by the bank	56.84

Additional information

On 24 October 2008 her cash in hand amounted to £265.96, and she had a bank overdraft amounting to £3519.06.

REQUIRED

Prepare the cash book for the week ended 31 October 2008. Balance the cash book. (20 marks)

plus 2 marks for presentation

■ ■ ■

Date	Details	Discount	Cash	Bank	Date	Details	Discount	Cash	Bank
24/10	Balance b/d		265.96		24/10	Balance b/d			3519.06
24/10	Sales		528.65		25/10	Compo	5.60		106.40
25/10	Mitchel Ltd	29.78		962.92	26/10	Drawings			120.00
27/10	Sales		745.88		27/10	Rent		80.00	
28/10	Bank C			600.00	28/10	Cash C		600.00	
28/10	Dishonoured cheque			73.87	30/10	Wages		567.34	
31/10	Balance c/d			2165.51	31/10	Interest			56.84
					31/10	Balance c/d		293.15	
		29.78	1540.49	3802.30			5.60	1540.49	3802.30
1/11	Balance b/d		293.15		1/11	Balance b/d			2165.51

Answer to question 4: candidate A

✐ This is a good answer. Only 2 marks are dropped. The dishonoured cheque should be in the credit bank column and the descriptions for the transfer from cash to bank are incorrect. Remember that descriptions tell the user of the accounts where the 'other' entry can be located. However, the dates and descriptions are awarded the other presentation mark. It is good to see that the candidate has not balanced off the two discount columns.

✐ **The candidate scored 20 out of 22 marks — a grade-A answer.**

Answer to question 4: candidate B

Date	Details	Discount	Cash	Bank	Date	Details	Discount	Cash	Bank
24/10	Balance b/d		265.96		24/10				3519.06
24/10	Cash sales		528.65		24/10	Compo	5.60		112.00
25/10	Mitchel	29.78		992.70	24/10	Private			120.00
27/10	Cash sales		745.88		27/10	Rent			80.00
28/10	Bank			600	28/10	Cash			600
28/10	Dishonoured cheque			73.87	28/10	Wages		567.34	
31/10	Balc/d			2821.33	31/10	Interest			56.84
					31/10	Bal c/d	24.18	973.15	
		29.78	1540.49	4487.90			29.78	1540.49	4487.90

The answer contains many basic errors. The transactions involving Mitchel and Compo are incorrect — the question clearly states the amounts that were paid and received. The description for drawings is not penalised, since the amount is correct and even though the description does not tell where the debit entry is, the principle is correct. The cash payment to bank incorrectly comes out of bank and is described incorrectly. It should also be written as 600.00, for clarity. The amounts are not penalised, but care should be taken as this type of careless entry can result in casting errors. The treatment of the dishonoured cheque is incorrect — it should be entered in the credit bank column. Rent has been entered incorrectly in the bank column. The discount column should not be balanced. Finally, a couple of marks are lost because all balances need to be brought down. One mark is scored for presentation as the dates are correct and the descriptions in the main are also correct.

Overall, the candidate scores 10 marks out of 22 and does not reach the standard required for a pass grade.

Q5 Question

The trial balance

Eric Hotler is a sole trader who owns a shop. The following information has been extracted from his books of account at 30 November 2008.

	£
Balance at bank	4 863
Bank loan repayable (2015)	25 000
Capital	12 244
Carriage inwards	453
Carriage outwards	656
Discounts allowed	830
Discounts received	1 008
Drawings	24 500
General expenses	18 769
Motor expenses	8 671
Purchases	167 919
Rent receivable	5 700
Returns inwards	275
Returns outwards	573
Sales	282 551
Stock 1 December 2007	18 434
Trade creditors	8 456
Trade debtors	1 763
Vehicle — at cost	32 000
— depreciation to date	8 000
Wages	64 399

REQUIRED

(a) Prepare a trial balance using the balances shown above. (11 marks)

(b) Explain the function of preparing a trial balance. (3 marks)

Additional information to the trial balance

(1) Stock at 30 November 2008 was valued at £18 648.

(2) During the year, Eric took goods from the business for his own private use valued at £300.

(3) Motor expenses due and unpaid amounted to £399 at 30 November 2008.

(4) Wages paid in advance amounted to £732 at 30 November 2008.

(5) Depreciation is to be provided on the vehicle at 25% using the straight-line method.

REQUIRED

(c) Prepare a trading and profit and loss account for the year ended 30 November 2008. (20 marks)

plus 2 marks for presentation

(d) Prepare a brief report addressed to Eric discussing the reasons why a trader should prepare a set of final accounts. (7 marks)

plus 2 marks for quality of written communication

questions & answers

Answer to question 5: candidate A

(a)

Trial balance at 30 November 2008

	Debit £	Credit £
Bank	4 863	
Bank loan		25 000
Capital		12 244
Carriage inwards	453	
Carriage outwards	656	
Discount allowed	830	
Discount received		1 008
Drawings	24 500	
General expenses	18 769	
Motor expenses	8 671	
Purchases	167 919	
Rent received		5 700
Returns inwards	275	
Returns outward		573
Sales		282 551
Stock	18 434	
Creditors		8 456
Debtors	1 763	
Vehicle	24 000	
Wages	64 399	
	335 532	335 532

This is a good answer. The heading is absolutely correct. The layout is clear and accurate except for the entry for vehicle; the depreciation should not have been deducted from the cost of the vehicle. Always show the asset at cost as a debit and the accumulated depreciation separately as a credit entry. Information should always be shown in full — accounting is a medium of communication. 10 marks are scored.

(b) A trial balance checks the arithmetic accuracy of all the entries in the ledgers and the cash book. It is also a great help when you have to prepare a trading and profit and loss account and balance sheet because you can get all the figures you need from one document.

This is a well-expressed answer. The candidate answers the question in the first sentence. The second sentence gives an additional use to which the trial balance can be put. Remember that there are no negative marks in any AS examination, so explain all written answers in as much detail as you know. If you write something that is incorrect, marks cannot be deducted from those that you have already scored.

(c)

Eric Hotler. Trading and profit and loss account for the year ended 30 November 2008

	£	£	£
Sales		282 551	
Returns		275	282 276	*wkgs*
Stock		18 434	
Purchases	167 619			*167 919 – 300*
Carriage in	453		
	168 072		
Returns out	573		
		167 499	
		185 933	
Stock		18 648	
Cost of sales		167 285	
Gross profit		114 991	
Rent		5 700	
Discount received		1 008	
Less expenses		121 699	
Discount allowed	830		
General expenses	18 769		
Motor expenses	8 272		*8 671 – 399*
Wages	63 667		*64 399 – 732*
Depreciation	8 000	99 538	*32 000 × 25%*
Net profit		22 161	

I have missed out carriage outwards. This should be an expense in the profit and loss account so my expenses should be £100 194 and my net profit should be £21 505.

🖉 This answer has a clear layout, using inset figures to give the answer clarity. There are good workings alongside the figures that have been adjusted. The only error is that the accrued motor expenses have been deducted rather than being added to the trial balance figure. However, because of the workings only 1 mark has been lost.

The candidate notices his/her own omission of the carriage outwards and makes a note to this effect. This is a good technique that will be rewarded. This type of note means that the original answer is not subject to many crossings out or alterations to figures that inevitably lead to further errors.

The quality of presentation scores both marks: the heading is perfect and all the labels are correct. This is a good answer that scores 21 marks out of a possible 22.

question 5

(d)

REPORT

To: Eric Hotler

From: A Student

Date: 4 December 2008

Subject: Reasons for preparing final accounts

Although you are not legally obliged to prepare sets of final accounts, I believe that it is in your best interest to prepare them.

✍ This is a good opening sentence that sets the scene and summarises the discussion that follows.

Accounts are prepared for two main reasons:

1   For management purposes. You can see what are the good financial points shown in the accounts and hopefully copy the good things into other parts of your business. You can also judge areas where economies might be made. For example, your motor expenses might include spending on petrol and your van may only be getting 4 miles to the litre. When you next change your vehicle you may find that your costs may go down if you buy a diesel vehicle which will give you more miles to the litre. You may also be able to get your purchases from a cheaper supplier. Are your wages too high? If so, you might be able to get rid of surplus staff. But do be careful that you don't upset the staff that are left.

   ✍ This paragraph is good and explains how Eric can manage his business more efficiently to save his business money. Although not expressed in perfect English, the candidate has communicated the information clearly and has given good examples.

2   For stewardship reasons. People who invest in a business are usually interested to see if you are using their finance wisely. They can only do this by looking at the final accounts. You have borrowed money long term from his bank. I am sure that the bank manager will want to see the accounts to make sure that his money is safe so that the interest can be paid on the loan and the loan can be paid back in 2015.

   ✍ This is another good paragraph. The candidate identifies a reason and develops it well using an example from the scenario of the question.

Although sole traders do not, by law, have to produce a set of final accounts it pays them to. Because the tax man and the VAT people might want to see the final accounts to prove how much you owe them.

   ✍ Although not written in excellent English, this is a valid observation, making it a sound answer that scores maximum marks — 7 marks for content plus 2 marks for quality of written communication.

🗩 **The candidate scores 43 marks overall — a grade-A answer.**

■ ■ ■

Answer to question 5: candidate B

(a)

Trial balance for the year ended 30 November 2008

	Debit £	Credit £
Bank	4 863	
Bank loan	25 000	
Capital	12 244	
Carriage in	453	
Carriage out		656
Discount allowed	830	
Discount received		1 008
Drawings		24 500
General expenses	18 769	
Motor expenses	8 671	
Purchases	167 919	
Rent	5 700	
Returns inwards	275	
Returns outwards		573
Sales		282 551
Stock	18 434	
Creditors		8 456
Debtors	1 763	
Vehicle	32 000	
Depreciation		8 000
Wages	64 399	
Suspense *(doesn't balance)*		35 576
	361 320	361 320

🗩 This response is badly laid out — none of the figures line up. Fortunately, the candidate has probably used a calculator to add each of the columns, so it is less important than if the calculation was done mentally. The candidate realises that the trial balance does not balance but has wasted time informing the examiner and calculating the difference in the two columns. The heading is incorrect and there are five errors — 8 marks scored.

(b) Trial balances that balance (unlike mine) prove that there are no mistakes in any of the ledgers. If the trial balance does balance they are very useful because you can just use the figures as a list to prepare your final accounts. The final accounts are the trading account, the profit and loss account, and the balance sheet. The

balance sheet is not really an account but you have to do one to prove that your final accounts balance.

🖉 The candidate has not answered the question. He/she makes an attempt in the first sentence, but the statement is not true (remember CROPOC). The candidate scores a mark for the observation that the trial balance can be used as a list from which to prepare the final accounts. The development is irrelevant to the question set.

(c)

Eric Hotler. Trading and profit and loss account for the year ended 30/11/08

	£	£
Sales	282 551	
Returns	573	283 124
Stock	18 434	
Purchases	167 919	
Carriges	1 109	
Returns	275	
	169 303	
Stock	18 348	
GP		132 769
Discounts		178
Rent	5 700	
Discount allowed	830	
General expenses	18 769	
Motor expenses	8 671	
Wages	64 399	
Depreciation	16 000	
NP		18 578

🖉 The layout here could be much better. The heading does not score, as the date is abbreviated. Both descriptions of profit need to be written out in full. The returns are confused. The goods for own use should be deducted from purchases (the candidate reduces closing stock by £300). Both carriages (spelled incorrectly despite appearing in the question) are added together and the inclusion of carriage outwards as an extraneous item means that an own figure for gross profit could not be rewarded. The netted discounts score 2 marks, but it is generally safer from a candidate's point of view to show them separately so there is no possibility of a casting error. The cost of sales figure is not identified and the rent received is treated as an expense. The aggregate depreciation is charged to the profit and loss account rather than only this year's provision. Despite all the errors, the candidate scores 11 marks.

(d) REPORT

To: Mr Hotler

From: A Student

Date: 4 December

Subject: Final accounts

Dear Mr Hotler,

I hope you are well. I am writing this report to you to tell you the reasons why you should prepare a set of final accounts.

> The first three lines of the report are superfluous and inappropriate to a report. They waste valuable time. The candidate should make relevant points immediately. In a report or a memorandum you may use bullet points, but remember that each point must be developed fully in order to gain maximum marks.

You really need to prepare a set of final accounts so that you can see how you are doing. Also it is the law that you must. If you did not know how you were doing you could overspend and go bust. It might tell you how you could improve your business. It could show you where you are wasting money.

> The candidate is touching on the management function of preparing a set of final accounts. It is not well expressed, although he/she states 'see how well you are doing' and 'how you could improve your business' and this is awarded 2 marks.

I hope that you have found my reasons of benefit to you. Please get in touch if you would like me to give you further advice.

I remain your good friend

A Student

> This is an inappropriate way to end a report. A brief summary and, if possible, a recommendation are the expected conclusions.

> **Overall this is a rather a weak set of answers, and not up to AS standard. However, there are indications that with more study and practice a much better mark could be achieved. 22 marks are awarded for the whole answer — just less than half marks.**

Verifying accounting records: correcting errors

The totals of Kurt Klinsmann's trial balance at 31 January 2009 did not agree. He entered the difference in the totals in a suspense account.

He has prepared a draft set of final accounts. These final accounts show Kurt's net profit as £43 714. On checking his books of account, he discovered the following errors.

(1) The purchases day book had been undercast by £100.
(2) A cheque paid for a van repair £937 had been entered on the credit of the bank column of the cash book as £973. No entry has been made in the general ledger.
(3) Rent £500 paid for November 2008 had been entered twice in the rent account.
(4) Discount allowed £139 had been entered in the credit of the discount received account as £193.

REQUIRED

(a) Make any entries in the suspense account to correct the errors. (7 marks)
(b) Calculate the corrected net profit after correcting the errors. (6 marks)
(c) Explain two types of error that are not revealed by preparing a trial balance. Give an example of each of the two types. (6 marks)

plus 2 marks for quality of written communication

■ ■ ■

Answer to question 6: candidate A

(a)

Suspense account

Rent	500	Purchases		100
Trial balance difference	905	Motor expenses		973
		Discounts *(139 + 193)*		332
	1405			1405

✎ Maximum marks are scored here. However, the candidate would have been safer showing that 'motor expenses' are made up of £937 and £36 as in the discounts entry. Remember to back up total figures with workings. Anything you have to key into your calculator should be shown in your answer.

(b)

	£
Profit as per draft accounts	43 714
Purchases	(100)
Motor expenses	(973)
Rent	500
Discount	(332)
Corrected net profit	42 809

This is a good answer that scores 5 marks. The candidate does not use a heading. Remember, headings tell the examiner what you are preparing. The only numerical error is to include the whole of the correction for the van repair. In fact, only £937 affects profit; the other £36 alters the bank balance, so it does not appear on the profit and loss account. Is this a genuine error or a transposition error because the figures are similar? Do take care when copying figures; transposition is so easy if you lose concentration.

(c) Complete reversal of entries is were, say, wages £500 is put on the debit of the cash book and in the credit of the wages account. Theres still a debit and credit using the same amount so it wont show up.

Original entry mistake like when £200 is put in the cash book for advertising instead of £20. £200 would go in the credit of the cash book and £200 would go in the debit of the advertising account in the general ledger.

Although the language is not perfect, the candidate clearly knows what the chosen types of errors are and gives two good examples. He/she scores maximum marks for content. Communication is good, but there are many spelling mistakes and poor grammar. Only 1 mark awarded for quality of written communication.

Overall, this is a clear grade-A answer scoring 19 out of 21 marks.

■ ■ ■

Answer to question 6: candidate B

(a)

Suspense account

Motor expenses	937	Purchases	100
Discount allowed	139	Rent	500
Discount received	193	Discount allowed	139
		Discount received	193
		Trial balance difference	337
	1269		1269

The candidate is unsure of basic double-entry principles and only scored a mark for the purchases correction and an own figure for the trial balance difference. Although the credit entries for discounts allowed and received are correct, both entries have been cancelled out by the same entries being made on the debit side of the account. Is the candidate hedging his/her bets? 2 marks are scored

(b)

	£
Profit as per draft accounts	43 714
Purchases	(100)
Motor expenses	(973)
Rent	500
Discount allowed	139
Discount received	(193)
New net profit	43 087

The candidate choses the incorrect amount for motor expenses but the effect of the adjustments to the purchases account and the rent account have been made accurately. The benefit of showing the two entries for the discount adjustment is clear in this answer. If the candidate had netted out the figures and used only one figure (£54), no mark could be awarded. Here, £193 scores a mark. The total gains an 'own figure' mark. 4 marks are scored.

(c) Reversal entries putting rent into expenses account doesn't make any difference the trial balance has got to balance.

Corresponding entries where two entries are the same like heating and lightning.

One type of error is identified and scores a mark, but the explanations and examples are unclear and imprecise. No further marks are awarded.

Overall, only 7 marks are awarded to this candidate, which would not earn a pass grade. It is clear that he/she should spend more time revising this topic.

Verifying accounting records: preparing control accounts

Brenda extracted a schedule of debtors for August from her sales ledger on 10 September.

The closing balance in the sales ledger control account at the end of August did not agree with the total of debtors for August, which was £14 371.
The following errors have now been discovered:
(1) The sales day book was undercast by £1000.
(2) £246 recorded in the sales returns daybook was actually returns outwards.
(3) Discounts allowed amounting to £461 have been totally omitted from the books of account.
(4) A cheque received from P Arker for £720 has been entered in Parker's account.
(5) A cheque received in July from Garibaldi for £93 has been dishonoured. It was entered in the cash book in August but not in Garibaldi's account.

REQUIRED

(a) Prepare the sales ledger control account after correcting the errors. (10 marks)
(b) Discuss the benefits that Brenda would gain from maintaining control accounts. (9 marks)

plus 1 mark for quality of written communication

■ ■ ■

Answer to question 7: candidate A

(a)

Corrected sales ledger control account — August

Sales	1 000	Discount allowed	461
Returns outwards	246		
Opening balance b/d	13 586	Balance c/d	14 371
	14 832		14 832
Balance b/d	14 371		

I have not recorded the P Arker entry because it is only an error of commission.

🖉 This is a good answer and scores 7 marks. The only error is that the candidate does not adjust the total of the schedule of debtors to include the unrecorded discounts and the dishonoured cheque; the closing balance should be £14 003 (14 371 – 461 + 93). It is good to see that the candidate refers to the P Arker entry (shown in italics). This dispels an examiner's fear that an item has been omitted because the candidate does not know how to adjust this error. The candidate earns a good mark for this testing question.

(b) Preparing control accounts will only disclose arithmetic errors in the ledger and in the control account. It will not show CROPOC errors which do not affect the balancing. So, someone looking at a control account that balances might think that it is bound to be absolutely correct. Also, a control account that does not balance tells the accountant that there is an error somewhere but not exactly where it is.

It will make the preparation of balance sheets much easier and much faster. This is because the control accounts show the total debtors and creditors at the end of every month.

It makes it much harder for people to fiddle the ledgers because the ledgers should be prepared by one person and the control account should be prepared by a senior member of staff.

I believe that Brenda should maintain control accounts because it will help to make sure that any errors in the ledgers are found and can be traced to a specific ledger.

✓ This is another comprehensive answer that covers the major points and earns 10 marks. Maximum marks are scored for content, with 1 mark for communicating the relevant points. Candidates must avoid colloquial expressions such as 'fiddle' and must not assume that examiners know what mnemonics stand for (e.g. CROPOC).

The candidate has also drawn the discussion to a conclusion in the final paragraph.

✓ **Overall, the candidate scores 17 marks — a grade-A answer.**

■ ■ ■

Answer to question 7: candidate B

(a)

Control account

Balance b/d	14 371	Discount allowed	461
Sales	1 000	P Arker	720
Parker	720		
Returns	246	Balances c/d	15 196
	16 337		16 377

✓ 4 marks are scored: 1 mark each for sales, returns, discounts and the error of commission. The candidate could have scored 1 extra mark by bringing the debtors down to start off September's control account. Remember, always bring balances down; an account is incomplete if you do not follow this simple step.

(b) If a control account balances it means that the entries into the ledger are correct.

You can see easily the balances for debtors and creditors so it makes the preparation of a balance sheet easier.

It will help to deter fraud.

🖉 The second two points score marks. The first line is not correct. The comment about the preparation of the balance sheet is succinct and scores 3 marks. An identification mark is awarded for the point regarding fraud, but this should have been expanded to explain how the preparation of control accounts can act as a deterrent. The candidate does not summarise the discussion. Although brief, the answer is awarded the communication mark.

🖉 **The candidate scores 9 marks overall, which is not sufficient to score a pass mark.**

Verifying accounting records: bank reconciliation statements

The bank columns in the cash book of Diveron plastics show a debit balance of £1768.37 on 30 November 2008. The balance shown on the business bank statement on the same date did not agree with the cash book.

On checking the cash book and bank statement, the following were discovered:
(1) A cheque paid to Bloggs, a supplier, for £123.50 had been entered in the cash book as £132.50.
(2) A cheque paid to the telephone company for £627.48 had been entered in the cash book but had not yet been presented to the bank for payment.
(3) The bank had paid Diveron's annual subscription to the plastics trade association by standing order for £220 on 23 November 2008. The subscription had not been entered in the cash book.
(4) Bank charges of £37.22 for a temporary overdraft in October 2008 had not been entered in the cash book.
(5) The bank had credited the account with bank interest of £7.61 on 30 November 2008. This amount had not been entered in the cash book.
(6) Cash and cheques amounting to £1278.09 had been entered in the cash book and paid into the bank on 30 November. These lodgements had not been entered on the bank statement.
(7) A cheque for £72.36 received from Harker and Co on 18 November 2008 was entered in the cash book on that date. The cheque has been dishonoured by Harker's bank on 29 November 2008. No entries have been made in Diveron's books of account.

REQUIRED

(a) Make the necessary entries in the cash book of Diveron plastics to bring it up to date on 30 November 2008. (8 marks)
(b) Prepare a bank reconciliation statement at 30 November 2008. (5 marks)
(c) Draft a memorandum to the owner of Diveron plastics explaining the importance of preparing a bank reconciliation statement. (6 marks)

plus 2 marks for quality of written communication

■ ■ ■

Answer to question 8: candidate A

(a)

Cash book bank columns only

Balance b/d	1768.37	Subscription	220.00
Bloggs	9.00	Bank charges	37.22
Interest	7.61	Dishonoured cheque	72.36
		Balance c/d	1455.40
	1784.98		1784.98
Balance b/d	1455.40		

This is a good answer, scoring all 8 marks. The heading is clear and all the descriptions are as required. The balance has been brought down.

(b)

Bank reconciliation statement at 30 November 2008

	£
Balance at bank from the updated cash book	1455.40
Add unpresented cheques	627.48
	2082.88
Less not on bank statement	1278.09
Balance at bank as per bank statement	804.79

Maximum marks are scored again. The heading is perfect and although some of the wording used is not standard, it is clear and unambiguous.

(c)

MEMORANDUM

To: the owner of Diveron plastics

From: A student

Date: 15 September 2008

Subject: Bank reconciliations

Doing a bank reconciliation checks the accuracy of the cash book entries for bank transactions. It shows where errors have been made like the mistake in entering Blogg's cheque.

It helps to update the cash book with items that the owner might have forgotten to enter in his cash book. Things like bank charges and standing orders. There are two examples in the case of Diveron: the subscription and the bank charges.

The bank reconciliation also checks the accuracy of the bank statement. Banks don't usually make mistakes but they could draw money out of the account by mistake or put someone else's money in.

☑ The content is awarded 5 marks. The candidate identifies three good reasons for preparing bank reconciliation statements. There could have been greater development in all three paragraphs by explaining how errors are located, how the subscriptions and charges are identified, and how withdrawals and deposits might end up in the wrong bank account. However, the candidate makes good use of examples taken from the question. Remember to identify a point, develop the point, and apply it to the question (remember IDA).

The memorandum format does not score as the subject is too vague. It should state 'the importance' or 'the benefits' of preparing a bank reconciliation statement. The remainder of the answer is well structured and clear, earning the further mark for communication.

☑ **The candidate earns 19 out of 21 marks overall — a grade-A answer.**

■ ■ ■

Answer to question 8: candidate B

(a)

Cash book

Dishonoured cheque	72.36	Balance b/d	1768.37
		Bloggs	9.00
		Telephone	627.48
		Subscription	220.00
		Charges	37.22
Balance c/d	2597.32	Interest	7.61
	2669.68		2669.68

☑ Only 2 marks are scored. The candidate confuses the opening debit balance in the cash book with a debit balance shown on a bank statement (indicating an overdraft). The subscriptions and bank charges are dealt with correctly. The unpresented cheque is included and this extraneous item means that the closing balance does not attract a mark. A mark could be scored if the closing balance is brought down to start off the cash book on 1 December 2008.

(b)

Bank Rec.

	£
Bank overdraft in cash book	(2597.32)
Unpresented cheque	627.48
Lodgement	(1278.09)
Bank statement balance	3247.93 overdrawn

This answer scores 4 out of 5 marks. Only the heading does not attract a mark. The candidate uses an own figure to start off the statement and, although the layout and descriptions are not perfect, the balance as per the bank statement is correct (using the cash book own figure).

(c)

MEMORANDUM

To: Diveron

From: Me

Date: 15 September 2008

Subject: Bank recs

It checks the cash book.

It prevents fraud.

It checks the bank.

The memorandum format does not score. As with candidate A, the subject of the memorandum is vague. Also, the 'From' line does not reveal the sender of the memorandum. Do not be tempted to be smart either, so do not use 'Batman' or 'Gordon Brown' unless these are your names. The content is too brief but scores 1 mark. To gain further marks the examiner must be convinced that the candidate does know what he/she is writing about. This can generally only be done if there is some good development.

A total of 7 marks is insufficient to gain a pass for this candidate.

Trading and profit and loss accounts and balance sheets

Fred Beare owns a general store. The following trial balance has been extracted from his books of account.

Trial balance at 31 December 2008

	Debit £	Credit £
Bank overdraft		19 614
Capital		79 916
Carriage inwards	617	
Carriage outwards	2 168	
Discounts allowed	412	
Discounts received		916
Drawings	39 400	
Equipment — cost	74 000	
— depreciation		37 000
General expenses	42 789	
Mortgage on premises		150 000
Motor expenses	13 628	
Premises at cost	200 000	
Purchases	326 490	
Rent and rates	9 500	
Returns inwards	1 380	
Sales		532 461
Stock at 1 January 2008	33 418	
Trade creditors		7 988
Trade debtors	6 480	
Wages	77 613	
	827 895	827 895

Additional information at 31 December 2008

(1) Stock was valued at £31 907.
(2) Rent and rates paid in advance amounted to £600.
(3) Wages due and unpaid amounted to £877.
(4) Equipment is to be depreciated at 10% per annum using the straight-line method.

REQUIRED

(a) Prepare a trading and profit and loss account for the year ended 31 December 2008. (22 marks)

plus 1 mark for quality of presentation

(b) Prepare a balance sheet at 31 December 2008. (13 marks)

plus 1 mark for quality of presentation

■ ■ ■

Answer to question 9: candidate A

Fred Beare. Trading and profit and loss account for the year ended 31 December 2008

	£	£	£
Sales			532 461
Returns inwards			1 380
			531 081
Less cost of sales			
Stock		33 418	
Purchases	326 490		
Carriage inwards	617	327 107	
		360 525	
Stock		31 907	328 618
Gross profit			202 463
Discount received			916
			203 379
Expenses			
Carriage outwards		2 168	
Discount allowed		412	
Wages		78 490	
Motor expenses		13 628	
Rent and rates		8 900	
General expenses		42 789	
Depreciation		740	147 127
Net profit			56 252

This is an excellent answer and earns 19 out of 22 marks. The layout is good and the candidate makes good use of insets, which help to show figures more clearly. There is, however, a lack of workings and this costs the candidate 2 marks. Two of the adjustments are made accurately and score 3 marks each. However, the candidate drops 2 marks for not showing the workings: £74 000 × 10% = £740 is obviously an error, but two components of the calculation are correct and would score. Remember, always show detailed working for all figures that require you to do a calculation. The examiner cannot see inside your head or calculator.

The presentation mark is awarded for clear labelling of the gross and net profit figures and the heading, plus the identification of the cost of sales figure.

(b)

Balance sheet at 31 December 2008

	£	£	£
Premises			200 000
Equipment		74 000	
Depn		37 740	36 260
Current assets			
Stock		31 907	
Trade debtors		6 480	
Prepayment		600	
		38 987	
Current liabilities			
Crs	7 988		
Bank o/d	19 614		
Accrual	877	28 479	10 508
			246 768
L T Liability			
Mortgage			150 000
			96 768
Capital			79 916
Profit			56 252
			136 168
Drawings			39 400
			96 768

This is an almost perfect balance sheet and earns the maximum **13** marks for content. However, the presentation mark is not scored, as the fixed asset heading is missing and 'long term' is abbreviated in the heading for the mortgage on the premises. Avoid the use of abbreviations: they can cost you marks. Again, there is a good use of insets. A subtotal showing the value of fixed assets would be useful. The depreciation of premises scores because the candidate uses his/her own figure from the profit and loss account to arrive at the aggregate depreciation figure.

Overall, this candidate scores 33 marks out of 37 — a grade-A answer.

■ ■ ■

Answer to question 9: candidate B

(a)

T & P & L a/c

	£
Sales	532 461
Rets in	1 380
	531 081
Stock	33 418
Purchases	326 490
Carriage in	617
Carriage out	2 168
Less stock	31 907
G P	200 295
Disc rec	916
	201 211
Less expenses	
Dis al	412
Wages	78 490
Motor expenses	13 628
Rent	9 500
Gen expenses	42 789
Depn	74 000
N P	17 608

✍ Although this answer has an unconventional layout, examiners are committed to rewarding correct content. Despite the poor presentation, this answer scores 15 marks. Much of the content is correct. A layout similar to that given by candidate A would make matters easier for both the candidate and the examiner. Carriage outwards is in the trading account and a couple of adjustments are not made. An own figure could score for the net loss, but the description is incorrect. No presentation mark is awarded — the heading is not as required and descriptions are not written in full. The cost of sales is not identified.

(b)

B/S for year end 31 December 08

Premises		200 000
Equip		74 000
Depn		74 000 ?
		200 000
CA		
Stock	31 907	
Drs	6 480	
Crs	7 988	
B/O	16 914	
Mortgage	150 000	
Capital		79 916
Profit		17 608
Drawings		39 400 *ran out of time*

 The candidate indicates that he/she has run out of time. In the time taken to scribble this, another item could have been put into the balance sheet that might have scored another mark. This candidate earns 6 marks. Three more marks could have been awarded if the candidate had classified the mortgage and had indicated whether the 'profit' and the drawings had been added or subtracted from the capital at 1 January 2008. The candidate does not score a presentation mark.

 Overall, 21 out of 37 marks are scored. Remember that an answer does not have to be perfect to score a pass mark or a grade A. The examiner wants to reward you for the knowledge and skills you have, not punish you for any mistakes. Candidate B scores a comfortable pass despite all the errors and inconsistencies, but could have done better by concentrating on layouts and stating whether items are added or subtracted.

Effect of errors on profit calculations

Derek Baines has prepared the following balance sheet for his business. Unfortunately, it contains several errors.

Derek Baines Balance sheet for the year ended 31 October 2008

Fixed assets			210 000
Current assets			
Stock		13 650	
Bank overdraft		2 500	
Bank loan due to be repaid in 2012		100 000	
Drawings		61 200	
		177 350	
Current liabilities			
Debtors	7 000		
Creditors	6 500	13 500	163 850
			373 850
Capital			108 350
Profit			74 500
Suspense account			191 000
			373 850

Additional information

- Wages amounting to £13 000 had been included in drawings.
- No entries had been made in the accounting records for the following transactions:
  (1) Fixed assets costing £34 000 had been purchased on credit.
  (2) Bad debts totalling £570 had been written off. No entries had been made in the accounting records.
  (3) A cheque for £650 had been dishonoured. No entry had been made in the accounting records.
  (4) Stock costing £750 had been sold on credit for £1000. No entry had been made in the accounting records.

REQUIRED

(a) Prepare a corrected balance sheet taking into account the additional information. (20 marks)

(b) Identify three types of error that might be present in the double-entry system which would not prevent a balance sheet from balancing. (3 marks)

■ ■ ■

Answer to question 10: candidate A

(a)

Derek Baines. Balance sheet at 31 October 2008

			£	
Fixed assets			244 000	*210 000 + 34 000*
Current assets				
Stock		12 900		*13 650 – 750*
Trade debtors		8 080		*7000 – 570 + 650 + 1000*
		20 980		
Current liabilities				
Trade creditors	40 500			*6500 + 34000*
Bank overdraft	3 150	43 650	(22 670)	*2500 + 650*
			221 330	
Long-term liability			100 000	
			121 330	
Capital			108 350	
Net profit			61 180	*74 500 – 570 – 13 000 + 250*
			169 530	
Drawings			48 200	
			121 330	

> This is an excellent answer and scores the maximum 20 marks. The balance sheet is well laid out and is supplemented by clear, accurate workings.

(b) There could be an error in the balance sheet that is cancelled out by an error in the profit and loss account. For example, the fixed assets could be added to a total that is £100 too much and in the profit and loss account the expenses could be underadded by £100. The balance sheet would still balance but there are two mistakes, one in the profit and loss account and one in the balance sheet, but it would not show up.

Also, the purchase of a fixed asset. The invoice for it is lost so it is not recorded as a purchase and it is not recorded as a creditor.

The profit and loss account could be added up wrong say £10 too much and the balance sheet could be added too much say the same £10. This would mean they would both balance.

> This question is a different take on the usual question regarding error not affecting the balancing of a trial balance. The marks allocated plus the word 'identify' should indicate to candidates that the answer requires a one word (or one brief phrase) for an answer. This candidate wastes time in writing in such detail. He/she would

have scored the same 2 marks simply by writing 'compensating error' and 'error of omission'. The third example given is a repeat of the compensating error.

✐ **Overall, this candidate earns 22 out of 23 marks — a comfortable grade-A answer (despite the poor grammar in (b)).**

■ ■ ■

Answer to question 10: candidate B

(a)

Balance sheet for Derek Baines at 31 October 2008

Fixed assets		244 000	
Current assets			
Stock	12 900		
Debtors	7 830		
	20 730		
Current liabilities			
Trade creditors	40 500		
Bank o/d	2 500	43 000	
Working capital (minus)		(22 270)	
		221 730	
Capital		108 350	
Profit		74 930	*74 500 – 570 + 1000*
		183 280	
Less drawings		48 200	
		135 080	

✐ This is a reasonable attempt that scores 12 marks. Showing more workings would have led to a higher score. Remember that any figure shown in the question that needs adjusting (no matter how simple the calculation appears to be) should always be backed up with workings shown on your answer booklet. Fortunately, the candidate does show workings for the profit figure.

(b) Addition errors.

Putting fixed assets under the heading of current assets.

Showing drawings as an expense in the profit and loss account.

All of these would still make the balance sheet balance.

✐ The second two points here are examples, but the question asks for *types of error* not examples, so no marks awarded.

✐ **The candidate scores 12 out of 23 marks overall, which would not earn a pass at AS.**

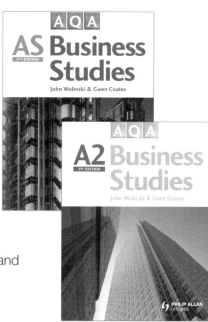

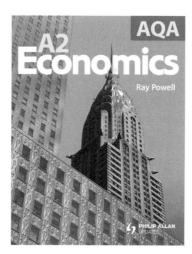